THE YORKIE DIARIES

THE YORKIE DIARIES

INNER THOUGHTS, SECRET ANTICS & TRUE CONFESSIONS

WILLOW CREEK PRESS

For Angie

© 2008 Willow Creek Press

Published by Willow Creek Press
P.O. Box 147, Minocqua, Wisconsin 54548

For information on other Willow Creek Press titles,
call 1-800-850-9453

Photo Credits: p2 © J. M. Labat/ardea.com; p5 © age fotostock/SuperStock ;
p6 © SuperStock, Inc./SuperStock; p8 © Juniors Bildarchiv/age fotostock;
p11 © J. M. Labat/ardea.com; p12 © Juniors Bildarchiv/age fotostock; p16 © Jerry Shulman;
p19 © Jerry Shulman; p28 © Richard Stacks/www.kimballstock.com;
p31 © Biosphoto / Klein J.-L. & Hubert M.-L./Peter Arnold Inc.;
p32 © Lynn D. ODellAnimalsAnimals; p35 © Mark McQueen/www.kimballstock.com;
p36 © Juniors Bildarchiv/age fotostock; p40 © Richard Stacks/www.kimballstock.com;
p43 © Isabelle Francais; p44 © Arco/C. Steimer/age fotostock; p47 © Isabelle Francais;
p49 © J. M. Labat/ardea.com; p50 © Phone-Auteurs Labat Jean-Michel/Peter Arnold;
p53 © Eunice Pearcy/AnimalsAnimals; p54 © Jerry Shulman/Superstock;
p57 © J. M. Labat/ardea.com; p58 © Richard Stacks/www.kimballstock.com;
p61 © Mark McQueen/www.kimballstock.com; p62 © Ron Kimball/www.kimballstock.com;
p69 © Ron Kimball/www.kimballstock.com; p75 © Ron Kimball/www.kimballstock.com;
p76 © Mark McQueen/www.kimballstock.com; p80 © Mark McQueen/www.kimballstock.com;
p83 © Ralph Reinhold/AnimalsAnimals; p87 © Ron Kimball/www.kimballstock.com;
p95 © Juniors Bildarchiv/age fotostock;

Printed in Canada

TABLE OF CONTENTS

INTRODUCTION

Who would have suspected that the darling little Yorkshire Terrier might have something to hide? Up until now we've assumed there's really not a whole lot going on in those pretty little heads. Well, now there's revealing new evidence that suggests otherwise. As it turns out, Yorkies are, get ready for this, diligent diary keepers. Yes, it's really true, Yorkies like to journal. A rash of Yorkie diaries has been uncovered lately (through an anonymous source), and while we thought it in poor taste to print the more shocking entries where identities would need to be disguised, we did get permission to reprint the following pages along with photographs of their authors.

SECRET
NAUGHTINESS

Monday, September 3rd

Dear Diary,

Today we practiced our two best faces. Freddie is getting really good at the teary, sad face we need to use when we have no excuse for our bad behavior. I, Miss Fancy, am an expert at the "I have no clue how this happened" face we use when there is still a question about our guilt. The new full-length mirror standing in the bedroom works great for our rehearsals. Hopefully we won't knock this one over too.

Fancy and Freddie

Friday, November 2nd

Dear Diary,

Today marks the end of another hard week perfecting my prima ballerina routine. Disciplined devotion is paying off (at least in treats) like crazy! It's well worth the tired feet! The bad news is, while I'm making out like a bandit, my little buddy Hannah is getting blamed for leaving her tutus lying around her bedroom floor. I can't resist pulling them out of the closet... they look so good on me.

Maya

Sunday, March 9th

Personal Journal Entry #27,

Everybody knows I'm a tough guy. Everybody. That goes for the intruder I caught in our house today who dared to squeak back at me when I tried to toss him out. I taught that stuffed shirt a thing or two about who has the last word around here, let me tell ya. You won't be hearing him squeak again anytime soon— I made sure of that. 'Cuz I'm tough. I really am. Yup.

Percy

Saturday, May 10th

Darling Diary,

How many hints will I have to give before someone
summons the portrait artist? Today I sat for hours,
poised and beautiful, in front of a stunning floral
arrangement just waiting for someone to notice how
wonderfully the colors offset my coat. Not only do I
have to put up with the total lack of artistic sensibility
in this family, but the lady of the house actually
demanded I remove myself from the furniture.
I guess not everyone has my flair for the avant garde.

Brigitte

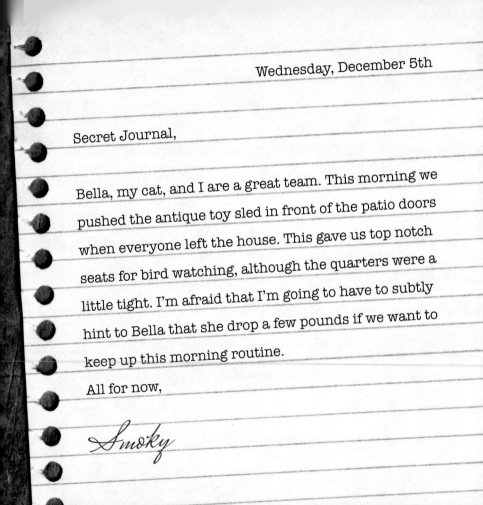

Wednesday, December 5th

Secret Journal,

Bella, my cat, and I are a great team. This morning we pushed the antique toy sled in front of the patio doors when everyone left the house. This gave us top notch seats for bird watching, although the quarters were a little tight. I'm afraid that I'm going to have to subtly hint to Bella that she drop a few pounds if we want to keep up this morning routine.

All for now,

Smoky

Thursday, April 19th

Hey Diary!

I taunted Charlie, our older dog, all day today! He's a lot bigger
than me and he keeps threatening to knock me for a loop.
Whatever. I pester him until he's ready to let me have it, then
I start crying super loud so someone comes running and gives
me the "poor baby" treatment and shoos the big dog away.
I can usually count on some cuddles and quality lap time after
that, while old Charlie sulks in the corner. I just try to make
sure I get taken everywhere the family goes...
I'm not too anxious to be left alone with the guy.
Bye for now,

Badger

Saturday, August 25th

Dear Journal,

I have a secret pact with Annie, my mom. Every time
we go to the café for our favorite grande-mocha-frappe-
whip-cream-puppy-upper treats and she decides to get
one of those mega chocolate chip cookies too, I have to
promise to keep this add-on to myself. I also have to be
on my best behavior if a really cute guy comes by.
I just wish I knew how to let her know when she has
cookie dough in her teeth.
Love,

Venti

Wednesday, June 6th

Dear Diary,

Day four with my new family. Tiger the cat is my pal.
Before I got here, he had the whole place to himself.
He's helping me fit in by giving me some pointers on
things to do around the house. They sound a little
naughty to me, but Tiger says I should trust him and
do what he says. Golly, a guy couldn't ask for a better
bud. So, my first task is to find a particular pair of red
high-heeled shoes and chew them into flats. Tomorrow
I will write all about how this worked out for me!

Moochy

Saturday, May 26th

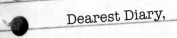

This is it... I'm in love. He may be a little out of my league but I don't care. I can't help myself. I see him strut by on his daily walk and I just lose all sense of propriety. He must be wonderful because today I heard his mom call him a great Dane, and he must like me too because she said Dane could have me for dessert if he wanted. I sure hope he invites me!

XOXOXOXOXOX

Fiona

Thoughts ON HAIR

Friday after school, 4/18

Dude,

I think I finally have the family convinced that no self-respecting two-year-old should be, like, all groomed and smelling good. I figure since I'm a teenager in people years, I deserve a little freedom to make my own appearance decisions. Besides, Jake (my 14-year-old human) won't hang out with me unless I'm a little crusty and he sure won't take me along if I'm wearing bows. He's teaching me this sweet trick. If you get the hair in your face perfectly arranged so that you can still sorta see and it doesn't get in your food, grown-ups pretty much don't bother you. Fur real.

Dusty

October 19... FRIDAY!

Dear Diary,

OMG!!! I LOVE my new haircut! Today at the doggy
spa my beauty expert Tina used her new organic
shampoo and conditioner, then styled this really
awesome flip into all my layers. I couldn't stop
smiling and yipping and running all over the place
when we got home. My mom invited all of her friends
over for her book club but I know she really just
wants to show me off. Gotta run next door to show
my BFF Bella... she is going to be soooo jealous! LOL!
BFN,

Brittany

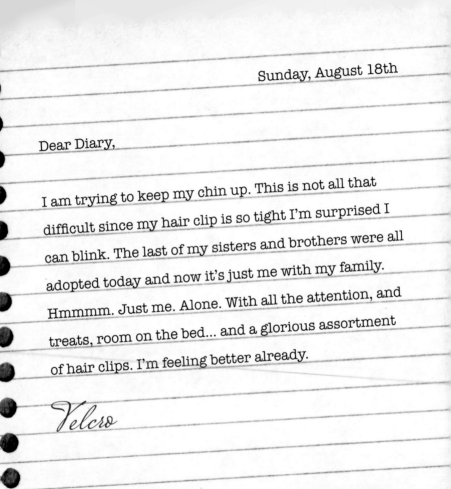

Sunday, August 18th

Dear Diary,

I am trying to keep my chin up. This is not all that difficult since my hair clip is so tight I'm surprised I can blink. The last of my sisters and brothers were all adopted today and now it's just me with my family. Hmmmm. Just me. Alone. With all the attention, and treats, room on the bed... and a glorious assortment of hair clips. I'm feeling better already.

Velcro

Dear Journal,

What a girl goes through to be her most beautiful self! I think my hair turns out best when I let it crimp dry in the sun... poolside of course. I learned a couple of great lessons today however. 1) Never attempt this on the pool boy's day off or you will be fetching your own refreshments. 2) Satisfy your thirst before removing your rollers or risk losing half your curl in the water bowl.

Princess

Day planner for 2007, side notes:

I don't get it. In my younger days everyone just called me Donnie. I'm a little older now, still dapper mind you, although the hair seems to have a mind of its own. Perhaps it's my sophisticated appearance that has prompted my new name because my family has taken to calling me "The Donald." They're also trying to teach me a new trick. I'm supposed to bark every time one of them says, "you're fired." I really don't get it.

Donnie

Monday, September 7th

Dear Diary!

There's a sneaky peeping tom cat lurking around our
yard. I have found (and tasted) evidence that he exists.
I think he was peering through the fence today when I
went out to... you know. So, while I used to complain
about the upkeep of my long locks, I now relish the
privacy they afford me. This is just shocking behavior!
Then again, he is a cat, and cats can be pretty creepy.

Bizzy

January 8, early morning

Dear Diary,

Today mom thought that if she put our food outside we
might run around looking for a tree trunk or a big rock to
wipe our faces on when we finished. We pretended we
were all cleaned up, then whimpered to come in. We both
dashed for the furniture. Nothing compares to the fringe
on the upholstered chairs when it comes to napkins. She
needs to be reminded from time to time that we have her
outsmarted two to one.

Spike and Poncho

April 15, Tuesday

Dearest Diary,

It's time to stir things up a bit here. I'm tired of tempering the terrier in me and down-playing my snarky, scurrilous side. Today I discovered the wonders of "hair gel." It has not only given me lift, but an unapproachable look that scares away less than considerate small children. I'm working on even more intimidating *Crouching Tiger, Hidden Dragon* type moves. I hope that someday I'll get the respect that I deserve (and that cool red kimono mom thinks would look so good on me).

Aiko

ON BEING A TERRIER

Saturday, June 23

Work Out Log, day 14 of training,

Limbered up at Pup-U-Up gym today getting ready
for our Musical Canine Freestyle dance tryouts.
I think, given just a few more basic obedience
trainings, my human will be ready to compete
with me. She's pretty good at following my lead.
Who knows, I might be the winner of Dancing
with the Dogs someday...

Calypso

Tuesday night, December 11

Journal,

I try never to start a fight but if I do, I'm sure
gonna finish it. This time I wasn't taking no for
an answer. My good-ole BIG plastic bowl is the
only dish I want my food in so I suggested that
the new fancy designer-decorated little finger
bowl be given to the cat. I'm no finicky eater and
I need something man-sized for those table
scraps. Jeez, you people.

Goliath

Dear Diary,

I don't know what to do. I want to play with the kids, even though they are rather slow learners when it comes to my rules. They don't get the part where we all chase the ball, but I'm the only one who's allowed to touch the ball. I guess I'll just have to keep giving them little "time outs" to remind them. That or I'll have to start some minor ankle biting. What part of "my ball" don't they understand?

Lightning

Saturday, July 21

Dear Secret Journal,

I HAD A BLAST TODAY! I learned all about the
park and picnics and long walks and ice cream.
I also learned that if you cry pathetically and
make very sad faces you can make good things
happen for yourself. I think I'll do that more
often. Yep, I sure learned a lot today! ☺

Metro

Dawg!

This is soooo much fun to do! I scoot out the back door,
or the kitty door, whatever works, and find a cool place
to hide. It doesn't take long for the whole family to join
in the game, calling and whistling for me, but I wait
until they start acting real crazy running around and
stuff, getting all frantic. Then I wait a little bit longer.
Then, BAM, I pop out of my hiding spot all excited!
Oh, the looks on their faces, too funny. Heh, heh...

Scampi

Monday morning, 5:00am

Dear Diary,

I know we're going for a ride today! I know it, I know it, I know it! So this morning I did what I always do when I can't stand the wait any longer. I put the fan next to the TV, turned on the nature channel, and got the next best thing to sticking my head out of the car window. Okay, but now it's time to get everyone up. I have places to go and strangers to bark at.

Chevy

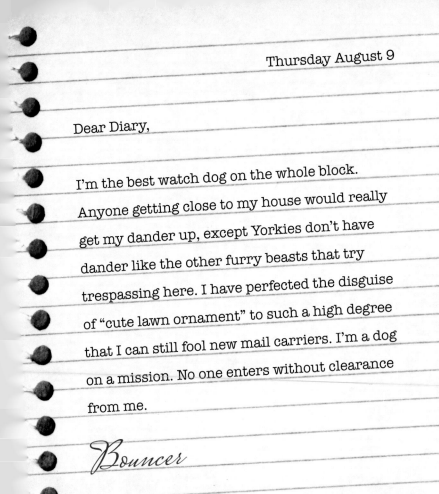

Thursday August 9

Dear Diary,

I'm the best watch dog on the whole block.
Anyone getting close to my house would really
get my dander up, except Yorkies don't have
dander like the other furry beasts that try
trespassing here. I have perfected the disguise
of "cute lawn ornament" to such a high degree
that I can still fool new mail carriers. I'm a dog
on a mission. No one enters without clearance
from me.

Bouncer

Sunday, nap time

Dear Dioree,

I wish everyone wud stop treating me like
a baby. I can do all kinds of stuff like the
big dogs.

Luv,

Doolittle

Thursday, December 20th

My Doggy Diary,

I taught my mom an important lesson today. Throwing something away from yourself means you don't want it anymore. Once an item is tossed, it then becomes the property of anyone who happens to find it, or run after it. Yep, you don't get to change your mind about keeping that toy. Boy, humans can be a nightmare to live with unless you enforce the rules.

Buster

The truth is I don't care which one of my parents takes me out, as long as I get to go along. I have to agree with dad that we really do look tough on his new bike. Hey, I wonder if that was part of the deal, dad gets the new ride as long as he gets me out from under mom's feet occasionally.
Hmmmm. Who cares, let's go!

Freeway

Saturday afternoon 5/3

Dear Diary,

Yesterday I heard dad ask mom if he was in the dog house again. Since we obviously do not have a dog house, I thought I'd get to work and surprise them both with a little addition in the backyard. Maybe now when mom asks dad where he's been, he won't seem so confused about his whereabouts. He can just say he was in the dog house, where else?

Andy

Notes for new horse training book:

The key to being a Yorkie Horse Whisperer is to tap into your natural alpha skills and larger-than-life attitudes. Remember, you are as big as you think you are. Take charge and every equine you encounter will be putty in your paws.

Dominique

Friday, October 26th

Yo Diary,

I really need to find the courage to voice my opinion on the sad state of dining affairs at this house. It's getting harder and harder not to lose it when the new chef, Pierre, presents one of his creations. We ain't exactly the haute dogs everybody thinks we are! Hey Frenchy! Save the fancy little portions for the rest of the family and grill us up a couple burgers.

Hank and Chuck

Wednesday, April 23rd

Dear Diary,

I sure wish my blog would catch on. I'm exhausted!
I never expected this would be such hard work.
I may have to take some time away from this for
awhile. In the meantime, I'll be checking back
every five minutes for any comments...

Posted by Nitro

Sunday, February 11

Dearest Journal,

I'm becoming quite concerned about Chewy. At first I thought it was cute when she started burying herself in stuffed animals after subjecting herself to constant replays of *ET*. It's become a bit of an addiction however. She strikes a pose and there is no getting her out of it. I think she may need help. I wonder if there's a support group out there for "Yorkies Who Are Movie-Obsessed." There must be others like her out there... gotta run we're watching *Star Wars* again!!!

Gizmo

Tuesday, January 16th

Victoria's Secret Diary,

I hope all of my secrets are safe with you! I have
found a perfect sleeping place. It's filled with
wonderful smells of my mom. She doesn't know
that I can open and shut this secret place all by
myself but she is wondering why her little
clothes in there are always warm and messed
up. She's been eyeing her boyfriend suspiciously
so I'm hoping I'm off the hook.

Vicki

Sunday, June 7th

All of my humans decided to head out to the lake today for a picnic. I was invited but acted disinterested. Who needs ants and sandy behinds? I'm planning a little picnic all my own with the cute little Yorkie down the street in the cool comfort of the air conditioning. I've never been one to suffer from separation anxiety!

Romeo

Saturday 10:00pm

Dear Diary,

I feel like a bit of a snoop but it sure is interesting
spying on mom and dad when they have people over.
They think I'm all snuggled in my bed tonight but
instead I found a great place at the top of the stairs to
check out all the fun. I'm kind of afraid to go down there
with all the dancing and everything. I might get
smooshed like that silly lampshade someone was
wearing. Oops, someone just knocked over a grape
juice. Glad it wasn't me this time! I better wake mom
up super early tomorrow so we can clean this up!

Martini

Dear Diary,

Snickers and I love to make mom and dad laugh. We do all kinds of silly and cute things to get them going! What's even better is our special bag of tricks we use to gross out the kids. One of our favorites is sharing our food... by licking each other's faces! Sometimes our tongues get in the way and everybody goes "eeeeuuuuuuh" all at once. It's great! And strangely pleasant. Hmmm.

Reuben

Sunrise, Monday, at the port of Los Angeles

Dearest Diary

All is lost forever. It has been revealed that it's actually
been me digging the narrow but amazingly deep hole in the
new lawn, not a gopher. I can't resist my innate instinct to
hunt for small rodents so I can't see how it's fair to punish
me, but dad has suggested that I be allowed to continue my
trip to China via the center of the earth. I prefer the "slow
boat" means of travel and have made arrangements
accordingly. I hope they take pity on me. If not, I bet
those freightliners will appreciate my hunting skills...

Virgil (The Verminator)

Sunday, March 18

Dear Diary,

I don't have much to record today since Twinkie
and I were forced to sit politely during tea at
grandma's house for most of the afternoon. Very
boring. I hope she appreciates how we suffered
through this long ordeal, but in order to guarantee
we're not invited back anytime soon, we both
decided to leave her little crumpets of our own on
the kitchen floor before we left. Tee hee indeed!

Dolly

Sunday afternoon, June 8th

Dearest Diary,

Here is the truest of truths. It's good to be the
queen. And, the truth be told, I do adore my silly
humans! I can't think of anything more wonderful
than just sitting in the grass on a splendid sunny
day watching them romp and toil about the yard.
It truly is a dog's life, and life is good.

Until next time,

Queenie